To Ellie, Enjoy the Opera! Liddy Lindsay

OPERA
A to Z

A Beginner's Guide to Opera

written and illustrated by Liddy Lindsay

published by Pinwheel Books

2013

Opera A to Z,
A Beginner's Guide to Opera
Copyright © 2013 Liddy Lindsay

Editor: Ashley Rumery
Proofreading: Anna Valutkevich
Layout and Cover Design: Nicole Gsell

This book was typeset with the fonts Didot and HelpUsGiambattista. The illustrations were created using watercolor.

Pinwheel Books
www.pinwheelbooks.com

Library of Congress Control Number: 2013936564
ISBN-13: 978-0-9854248-3-1

To my children, Milton and Lavinia,
who always seemed to enjoy the opera

To opera lovers, wherever you are...

*

In memory of my mother Peggy
who instilled in me the love of art and culture,
and with whom I attended countless operas

*

Many thanks to:

Cynthia Eiseman for her editorial guidance;

Charlotte Petsopoulos, my dear friend and agent, for
helping me promote *Opera A to Z*
from my studio to opera houses near and far;

Sylvia Westphal, my Nonquitt friend, for making this
book possible.

INTRODUCTION

Opera A to Z: A Beginner's Guide to Opera introduces the uninitiated, young and old alike, to an enticing array of operatic works. **Opera** is an art form that combines music, called a **score**, with text, called a **libretto**, into a single work, performed on stage. Musicians and singers, who are also actors, work together to perform the opera. On each page you will find the description of a classic opera, under its original name, that corresponds to a letter of the alphabet. Character names are listed in the original language whenever possible. For each opera you will find a picture that shows a scene, song or character from the opera. Sets, costumes and other elements work in tandem with the music and words to produce an opera. The images in this book are meant to provide an immediate visual experience like the sets and costumes do in a live opera. Look for the letter in the composition of each picture!

On some pages you will find extra information that explains a part of the story or provides more context for understanding it. This information is listed under the heading "aside." In opera, an aside is when one character in the opera speaks directly to the audience to tell them something the rest of the characters cannot hear. In a similar way, the asides in this book are meant to be things that the author tells you apart from the main story.

You have probably had much more experience with opera than you think. Musicals, on stage or in film, developed directly out of the operatic tradition. In fact, you may have heard music from some famous operas without even realizing it. Opera music has made its way into film, television, sporting events and other elements of our modern culture. If these exciting stories of love, betrayal, friendship and adventure spark your interest, there are resources in the back of the book to help you learn more.

THE FOUR MAJOR ERAS: Baroque, Classical, Romantic and Modern/Twentieth-Century

Opera began in Italy in the late fifteen hundreds at the very end of the Renaissance, a time of artistic renewal in Europe. In 1598 a Roman musician, Jacopo Peri (1561-1633), collaborated with a poet to write the first opera, *Dafne* (Daphne). Only small pieces of it survive. This early opera was like a play set to music. It featured **recitative** rather than the elaborate singing we now associate with opera. Recitative is a sort of sing-talking that can range from rhythmically spoken words to words spoken melodically, similar to singing. *Dafne* probably featured more of the former. As much of this very early opera is lost to history, the earliest operas that are still performed today developed during the **Baroque** (*ba*-**roke**) era.

The Baroque period began in 1600 and lasted roughly until 1750. During this time, art, architecture and music became more detailed and elaborate. A sense of grandeur and lavishness became associated with the period and its artistic works. All over Europe, strains of opera were developing. In Italy, Claudio Monteverdi (1567-1643) composed operas that used recitative and incorporated **arias**, or expressive melodies usually sung by one person. Arias soon became an integral part of opera. By George Frederic Handel's time (1685-1759), arias had largely replaced recitative. Orchestras during the early part of the period were small, and often featured a **harpsichord**, an instrument with strings inside that the player plucks by pressing a keyboard. It is like a piano, but with a different sound. Later in the era, orchestras grew as instruments developed. During the Baroque period, there was a great deal of variation in operatic styles. Two major styles were **opera seria** and **opera buffa**. *Opera seria* refers to serious operas usually based on mythology, religion or other such topics. *Opera buffa* refers to operas with more lighthearted or comic themes. As the name suggests, they often included old buffoons, characters like clowns or jesters that bore the brunt of the comedy.

By the seventeen hundreds, opera began to include more compositions for a **chorus**, or a group of singers, and reintroduce recitative elements that had fallen out of fashion. This marked the **Classical** era, from 1750 to about 1830. The composers of this time balanced instrumental music and singing. Many of the operas that are still popular today are from this period. The famous Wolfgang Amadeus Mozart (1756-1791) composed during this time. The genre of **grand opera** developed during his lifetime. As the name suggests, these operas were grander than ever before, with more elaborate compositions, larger orchestras and fancier costumes. They could even feature ballet and sometimes included recitative elements on the more melodic end of the spectrum.

The spectacular operas of the Classical era gave way to more streamlined operas during the **Romantic** era starting in 1830 and continuing until 1900. The intellectual and cultural movement of the period valued artistic beauty. During this time, the term **bel canto**, which means "beautiful singing," became attached to opera. This term has many meanings, but commonly refers to complicated melodies that singers could embellish with their own flourishes, combined with musical numbers to create scenes. Gioachino Rossini (1792-1868) is often considered to have composed bel canto operas.

MOZART

PUCCINI

VERDI

WAGNER

6

Drame lyrique, or **lyric drama**, also characterized this time. Lyric drama was a simplified version of grand opera. It preserved some of the more melodic recitative and streamlined the lavish musical numbers. At the end of this era, a genre known as **verismo** (*ve-rees-mo*) emerged. Composers in the late eighteen hundreds and early nineteen hundreds integrated values of the Romantic era with the realities of the modern times to create *verismo*. These operas featured relatable characters in a realistic setting. Until this time most operas covered themes of mythology in hallowed halls or betrayed royalty in rambling palaces. Characters were nobles, clergy and even gods rather than common people in common situations. This genre extended into the twentieth century.

As the twentieth century dawned, opera and other art forms became more contemporary. The great Giacomo Puccini (1858-1924) is part of the **Modern/Twentieth-Century** era, from 1900 until the present day. Some early modern composers were very Romantic in character, like Puccini, and could be considered late Romantic while others veered from the tradition like Samuel Barber (1910-1981). The millennium brings with it new musical developments — opera continues to evolve today.

THE FOUR GREAT COMPOSERS:
Mozart, Puccini, Verdi, and Wagner

Pictured on the four corners of the preceding page are the mainstays of the Grand Opera tradition: Wolfgang Amadeus Mozart, Giacomo Puccini, Giuseppe Verdi and Richard Wagner. They are portrayed in **grisaille** (*gris-eye*), an artistic technique that uses shades of grey to create a three-dimensional effect in a two-dimensional medium. It can make a painting look like a marble sculpture. This technique was used widely when these composers lived.

In the upper left corner is Wolfgang Amadeus Mozart (1756-1791), one of the most famous and prolific composers. Mozart lived and worked during the seventeen hundreds, a time of great operatic development. Mozart bridges the Baroque and grand opera traditions. His early operas fall into the style of *opera seria*. These operas, like *Idomeneo*, are a hallmark of the Baroque period. Later he wrote grand operas like *Die Zauberflöte*. These grand operas can generally be performed with a period orchestra like one that would have originally performed them, or with a full modern orchestra, without losing any major musical qualities. Mozart wrote operas for people of all social classes: the nobility, the clergy and the middle class that emerged at the end of the seventeen hundreds. Because he wrote for such a wide audience in his time, his operas reached, and continue to reach, people from different backgrounds.

Giacomo Puccini (1858-1924) is in the upper right corner. Puccini's operas feature some of the most beloved **duets,** or songs sung by two people, and arias that are still performed around the world in all types of venues. For many ardent fans it was the music of Puccini, whether a snippet of an aria or a complete performance, that ushered them into the magical world of opera. His music has made its way into popular culture at sporting events, in television commercials and movies. "O mio babbino caro" ("Oh, My Beloved Daddy") from his opera *Gianni Schicchi*, for example, has been covered by contemporary Classical singers and has even been featured in video games.

Giuseppe Verdi (1812-1901) and Richard Wagner (1813-1883) are depicted respectively in the lower left and right corners. They are painted on the same line because they were contemporaries and rivals who composed some of the most seminal operas of the grand opera repertoire. Their works were compared to each other. Verdi, in particular, was accused of mimicking Wagner.[1]

Through his music, Verdi captured the heart and soul of his compatriots at the time of the unification of Italy, under the king whose initials spelled out VERDI, "Vittorio Emanuelle, Rei d'Italia" ("Vittorio Emanuelle, King of Italy"). He made social statements in his music that helped push his views of society forward, such as glorifying a courtesan in his opera *La Traviata (The Fallen Woman)*, when much of society would look down upon a character in this position. Even though Verdi's music inspired the birth of modern Italy, he wrote several works about different cultures such as the one featured in this book, *Aida*.

Like Verdi, Richard Wagner was an important national figure whose works became part and parcel of his German culture. He brought to life German mythology in the form of *Der Ring des Nibelungen*, the *Ring Cycle*, an epic set of operas including *Die Walküre (The Valkyrie)*. His long operas enraptured his native Germany but were not without critics. The thunderous music and beautiful lyricism resounded like a battle cry when Germany was expanding in the nineteen hundreds. Yet, his operatic contributions go beyond national appeal like the works of the other composers mentioned here.

Mozart, Puccini, Verdi and Wagner are heard around the timeless musical universe. These masters are just four of the influential composers featured in *Opera A to Z*. Each has left his mark on opera. Though written in different languages throughout the centuries, opera's power transcends language and resonates throughout time so we can still enjoy it today. Lucky us!

Every letter has a story.

It starts with "Aïda"
and ends with "Zauberflöte,"
both set in Egypt.

But every culture and continent in
between is included.

AIDA
by Giuseppe Verdi

b. October 10, 1812 in Le Roncole, Italy
d. January 27, 1901 in Milan, Italy
Premiered in 1871

Aida (*aye-ee-dah*) is a famous tale of love and betrayal set in ancient Egypt when the Egyptians were fighting the Ethiopians. Aida is an Ethiopian princess enslaved by the Egyptians. Aida is in love with Radames, the Egyptian war hero who has just vanquished her people. Unfortunately, the Egyptian princess Amneris is in love with him too.

After Radames' victory march, the warriors parade the Ethiopian captives to showcase their triumph. Aida sees her father Amonasro, the king of Ethiopia, among the captives. She meets him in prison where he entreats her to extract military secrets from Radames so he can pass them on to the Ethiopian fighters.

Later Aida and Radames have a secret rendezvous. After affirming their love for each other, Aida gets Radames to divulge the plans for the forthcoming battle. He realizes too late that he has betrayed his country by doing so.

In the meantime, Amneris grows suspicious of Aida and Radames. Secrets begin to unravel. Amneris discovers Aida's royal identity and Radames' betrayal. The Egyptian authorities sentence him to death.

Radames is sealed in a pyramid to starve. As he laments his fate — to die alone, no food, no water, no Aida — he hears a voice from the shadows and realizes it is she! She has snuck into the tomb so they can die together, sealed forever.

Aside: Verdi composed Aida in 1869 but it did not premiere until 1871 because the Franco-Prussian War broke out in Europe. It was supposed to premiere in the new opera house in Cairo, Egypt, but the costumes were all made in France. In 1870, the city of Paris was under siege by the German kingdom of Prussia, and so were the costumes! The production could not happen until the following year.[2]

10

MADAMA BUTTERFLY
by Giacomo Puccini

b. December 22, 1858 in Lucca, Italy
d. November 29, 1924 in Brussels, Belgium
Premiered in 1904

The tragic *Madama Butterfly (Madame Butterfly)* takes place in Nagasaki, Japan. Here, the American naval lieutenant Benjamin Franklin Pinkerton decides to buy a young Japanese bride from a marriage broker named Goro. The bride is named Cio-Cio-San (**cho**-*cho-san*), known as "Butterfly." Even though Butterfly's family will disown her if she marries him, she accepts the arrangement and falls in love with him.

Pinkerton leaves soon after their wedding, promising to return. He has unknowingly left Butterfly pregnant with a son she names Dolore (*doh*-**lo**-*reh*), which means "pain" or "trouble". She waits for years for Pinkerton to return, caring for herself and Dolore with her loyal servant Suzuki. Food, fuel and money grow scarce. Suzuki appeals to Sharpless, the American consul, for help. Goro, trying to help, offers another marriage proposal to Butterfly. She refuses and declares her love for the distant lieutenant.

Sharpless comes to visit Butterfly to read a letter with bad news: Pinkerton is returning to Nagasaki, but with an American wife. When he sees how excited Butterfly becomes upon learning of Pinkerton's return, he cannot bear to finish the letter.

The innocent Butterfly spies Pinkerton's ship in the harbor and prepares for his arrival. She is elated! Pinkerton arrives at the house with the official Mrs. Pinkerton, but soon realizes his mistake and leaves. Butterfly encounters not her beloved lieutenant, but his new wife. Shattered, she sends Dolore out of the house and kills herself with her father's knife.

Mme Butterfly - Puccini

CARMEN
by Georges Bizet

b. October 25, 1838 in Paris, France
d. June 3, 1875 in Bougival, France
Premiered in 1875

Carmen is the passionate tale of a beautiful gypsy who works in a cigar factory in Seville, Spain. It is an **opéra comique,** or comic opera, an opera that is tragic or comedic but with some spoken dialogue and arias. Carmen is arrested for trying to slash a co-worker with a knife. Don José, a soldier, is in charge of detaining and imprisoning her. "Don" is a title that refers to someone with social standing. Carmen sings him a provocative song, asking him to free her. Mesmerized, he does. Carmen escapes and Don José is arrested for letting her go.

Up until he met Carmen, Don José had been honorable and hard working. Once Carmen bewitches Don José, he is never the same. As soon as he is released from jail, he heads straight for the tavern to find Carmen. When he finds her, she dances for him and he deserts the army.

Don José now joins a gang of gypsy tobacco smugglers. As Don José begins to regret what he has done, Carmen starts getting bored of him and tells him to go back home. Meanwhile the dashing bullfighter Escamillo appears, declaring his love for Carmen. The two men fight, and Escamillo leaves, but not without first inviting everyone to his next bullfight. José then learns that his mother is ill, so he ends up having to leave, vowing to come back and find Carmen wherever she is.

Carmen soon becomes Escamillo's muse. Beautifully dressed, she rides to the bullfight in a gorgeous carriage with an entourage of her gypsy companions. One of them spots Don José in the crowd and warns Carmen, who decides to go find him. That is a fatal mistake. Don José stabs her, blaming her for ruining his life. If Carmen will not be with him, he will not let her be with anyone.

Aside: You may have heard some of the music from *Carmen* before. The opera's **habanera,** a rhythmic dance song that originated in Cuba, "L'amour est un oiseau rebelle" ("Love is a Rebellious Bird"), and "Couplets du Toréador" ("Toreador's Song") are both very popular. When many people think of opera, the *habanera* that Carmen dances is what comes to mind.

Le jeux font fait pour danser

DAPHNE
by Richard Strauss

b. June 11, 1864 in Munich, Germany
d. September 8, 1949 in Garmisch-Partenkirchen, Germany
Premiered in 1938

Daphne is a tragic opera based on a Greek myth, set in ancient times. Daphne is the beautiful young daughter of a fisherman and loves nature above everything else. Her childhood friend Leukippos, now a young man, is in love with her. She says she only loves him like a brother.

All the families in the village are getting ready for the festival of Dionysus, a wild party in honor of the god of wine and madness. Daphne's father Peneios wishes for a god to come from Mount Olympus and bless the event. Soon, a tall handsome stranger turns up dressed as a herdsman. It is the god Apollo! Peneios asks Daphne to look after the stranger. When Apollo sees Daphne, he falls in love. He confesses his feelings to the beautiful girl, but Daphne gets scared and turns him down.

The festival procession and dancing begin. Daphne's old friend Leukippos has disguised himself with one of Daphne's dresses and, pretending to be a girl, asks her to dance. Apollo sees this and becomes furious. He interrupts the festival and accuses Leukippos of trying to deceive Daphne. Leukippos declares his love for Daphne and asks her to marry him. Jealous, Apollo reveals his identity as well, and when Daphne refuses both of her suitors, Apollo fatally wounds Leukippos with an arrow.

When Apollo sees how he has upset Daphne by killing her lifelong friend, he is overcome with regret. He wants to make amends for straying outside the realm of the gods and mixing with mortals. He asks Zeus, the most powerful god, to turn Daphne into a laurel tree so she can become one with nature.

Aside: The sculpture that inspired the "D" on the facing page is Gian Lorenzo Bernini's profound interpretation of the moment when the gods turn Daphne into a tree. This sculpture "Apolo e Dafne," created between 1622 and 1625, is at the Villa Borghese in Rome, Italy.

DAPHNE

L'ELISIR D'AMORE

by Gaetano Donizetti

b. November 29, 1797 in Bergamo, Italy
d. April 8, 1848 in Bergamo, Italy
Premiered in 1832

L'Elisir d'Amore (The Elixir of Love) is one of the happy operas of the lyric repertoire. Nemorino, an earnest young peasant, loves the beautiful maiden Adina, who is oblivious to him. Army sergeant Belcore and his men arrive into town, and Belcore asks Adina to marry him. She says she will think about it.

A quack doctor, Dulcamara, comes through town selling potions and Nemorino asks if he might have a love elixir — a potion that promises love at first sight. Dulcamara says yes, and Nemorino spends all his money on the elixir, hoping that Adina will fall in love with him after he drinks it. In reality, however, the elixir is only wine.

Nemorino drinks the whole bottle, and gets drunk. When he sees Adina next, he acts foolishly, as if he did not care for her. Adina in response starts flirting with Belcore, and agrees to marry the sergeant.

Desperate, Nemorino asks the doctor for another bottle of the elixir. Nemorino has no money left, and the doctor says he will wait for Nemorino to borrow money from someone in order to buy the elixir. Sergeant Belcore tells Nemorino he can be paid money by enlisting in the army, so Nemorino signs the papers, gets paid, and buys another bottle of wine (thinking it love elixir) from the quack doctor.

Meanwhile, news arrives that Nemorino's rich uncle has died, leaving him a fortune. Nemorino does not know this yet, but the girls from town do, so they suddenly start paying him attention. Adina looks at the flirting girls jealously, and Nemorino notices a tear on her cheek — *una furtiva lacrima*. He realizes she loves him after all! Adina buys back Nemorino's army contract and confesses that she is in love with him. The quack doctor Dulcamara goes around town telling people how his elixir can make people fall in love and become rich.

Elisir
d'Amore

The luckiest guy in opera, NEMORINO, has a bit of love potion, scores Adina his ♥ gets, dodges Army.

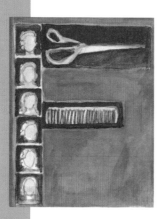

FIGARO (character) in –

Il Barbiere di Siviglia by Gioachino Rossini
b. February 29, 1792 in Pesaro, Italy
d. November 13, 1868 in Passy (Paris), France
Premiered in 1816
-and-
Le Nozze di Figaro by Wolfgang Amadeus Mozart
b. January 27, 1756 in Salzburg, Austria
d. December 5, 1791 in Vienna, Austria
Premiered in 1786

There are two operas about Figaro, a central character of the Age of Enlightenment. This was a time during the sixteen and seventeen hundreds when reason and science were becoming more important than religion in thinking, art and culture.

The painting on the facing page shows Figaro, the barber and matchmaker of Seville, on the steps of his barbershop. On the top floor we see Rosina and her maid. In *Il Barbiere di Siviglia (The Barber of Seville)*, Figaro contrives for Count Almaviva to marry Rosina, saving her from her guardian Bartolo, a doctor who wants her for her money. Because Figaro successfully arranges the marriage between the Count and Rosina, Count Almaviva owes Figaro a favor.

In *Le Nozze di Figaro (The Marriage of Figaro)*, the Count allows Figaro to marry Rosina's maid Susanna, even though Count Almaviva himself wants to be with her. The Count's housekeeper Marcellina wants Figaro to marry her instead. Then it is discovered that Marcellina is Figaro's mother, and the doctor Bartolo is Figaro's father. Marcellina and Bartolo marry and Figaro is free to marry his beloved Susanna.

Meanwhile, Rosina (now Countess Almaviva) is sad that her husband does not love her anymore, and that he wants to be with Susanna. But Susanna and Rosina conspire to trick the count into acknowledging that he actually loves Rosina. The women exchange clothes and when the Count sees "Susanna" (really Rosina) he showers her with love. When the Countess reveals her identity, the Count realizes he does love his wife and asks for her forgiveness.

Aside: The 1950 cartoon "The Rabbit of Seville" by famed Looney Tunes director Chuck Jones uses Rossini's **overture** to *Il Barbiere di Siviglia* and features Bugs Bunny singing variations of this opera. An overture is a song that the orchestra plays at the beginning of an opera that usually contains parts of all of the songs featured. Other cartoons of this era feature music from this opera as well.[3]

Figaro, Barber of Seville, arranges ♥ between Count Almaviva
& Rosina. Figaro becomes the butler & Susanna. 2 operas, Le Nozze &

DON GIOVANNI
by Wolfgang Amadeus Mozart

b. January 27, 1756 in Salzburg, Austria
d. December 5, 1791 in Vienna, Austria
Premiered in 1787

Don Giovanni is the story of a notorious low-level nobleman based on the legendary Don Juan Tenorio, a courageous but hopelessly womanizing character. The opera is famous for blending comedic and dramatic elements and for its compelling title character. Set in Seville, Spain, during the sixteen hundreds, it opens with Don Giovanni's servant Leporello complaining about having a master who gets into so much trouble.

Leporello is waiting for Don Giovanni to come out of the house of Donna Anna, an engaged woman. As Don Giovanni tries to escape, Donna Anna's father hears her cries and confronts him with a sword. Don Giovanni fights back and kills him. Now Donna Anna's fiancé, Don Ottavio, swears to seek justice.

Later they encounter another woman, Donna Elvira, who has also been a victim of Don Giovanni. Don Giovanni escapes yet again as Leporello distracts Donna Elvira by reading an enormous scroll of Don Giovanni's conquests. There are thousands of women of all social classes and nationalities on the list! Meanwhile, Donna Anna and Don Ottavio, her fiancé, are in hot pursuit of Don Giovanni to seek justice. But once again he eludes them. Don Giovanni notices Zerlina, a pretty peasant girl about to get married to Masetto. Donna Elvira, Donna Anna and Don Ottavio thwart his attempt to seduce her.

Undeterred, Don Giovanni spots Donna Anna's handmaiden and tries to seduce her instead. To throw the others off his trail, he swaps clothes with Leporello. Meanwhile Leporello feels the wrath of the three in pursuit of his boss.

Finally, Don Giovanni's deeds catch up with him. In a cemetery, a statue of Il Commendatore ("Knight Commander"), Don Pedro, Donna Anna's deceased father, warns Don Giovanni about the danger of his ways. Don Giovanni makes Leporello invite the statue to dinner. When the Commendatore arrives in statue form, he reverses the invitation and invites Don Giovanni to dinner. Don Giovanni blithely accepts the dinner offer without realizing that this is not a dinner for the living, but the dead. The Commendatore demands that Don Giovanni repent or be damned. Don Giovanni refuses, and the fires of hell consume him. The victims of his antics – Donna Anna, Don Ottavio, Donna Elvira, Zerlina, Masetto and Leporello – live to tell the tale.

Don

GIOVANNI

Leporello, Don Giovanni's servant lists his master's conquests to Elvira.

HÄNSEL UND GRETEL
by Engelbert Humperdinck

b. September 1, 1854 in Siegburg, Germany
d. September 27, 1921 in Neustrelitz, Germany
Premiered in 1893

Hänsel and Gretel is a **fairy tale opera**, a category for operas that are based on fairy tales. Hänsel and Gretel are two children who live in a cabin in the woods with their father and mother (or stepmother in some versions). Their father is a poor broom-maker. There is little food in the house and everyone in the family has to work hard and contribute to the household. While their parents are away at work, Gretel is in charge of doing the housework and encourages Hänsel to help.

Gretel tries to make the chores more like games, so while she and Hänsel are dancing around they accidentally spill the milk meant for the family's dinner.

Tired from work, their mother arrives home and sees the spilled milk. Furious, she punishes the children and sends them out to the woods to collect strawberries. Night is falling and their father comes home. As he sits down after a hard day, he realizes Hänsel and Gretel are nowhere to be found. Their mother remembers she sent them out to collect food. She does not know that there is a witch in the woods.

Hänsel and Gretel's parents rush out to find them in the night. Meanwhile, deep in the forest, hungry and tired, Hänsel and Gretel fall asleep. Fourteen angels spread sleep dust on them and protect their sleep.

After they wake up they continue down a path in the woods that leads to a candy house surrounded by a fence made of gingerbread children. When they are breaking pieces of candy off the house the witch comes out and traps them. She locks Hänsel in a cage to fatten him up so she can bake him and forces Gretel to be her servant. She decides to teach Gretel how to make cakes. When she checks to see if Hänsel is fat enough to bake, he sticks a twig out rather than his finger and tricks her into waiting. In the meantime, Gretel breaks the juniper branch that the witch uses for her magic and releases Hänsel. When the witch asks her to check on the cakes in the oven, Gretel pretends to be ignorant so the witch has to open the door for her. Taking their chance, the children push the witch into her own oven.

Destroying the witch breaks the spell on the gingerbread children and they return to life. Hänsel and Gretel's parents follow the noise and commotion to the candy house. They reunite with the children in a house full of food.

IDOMENEO
by Wolfgang Amadeus Mozart

b. January 27, 1756 in Salzburg, Austria
d. December 5, 1791 in Vienna, Austria
Premiered in 1781

Idomeneo (ee-doe-meh-nay-o) is one of Mozart's great operas in the **opera seria** style, written just as that style was starting to fall out of favor. It is the story of Idomeneo, the king of Crete, a Greek island, around the time of the mythological Trojan War.

While Idomeneo is on his way back from Troy, Idomeneo's boat sinks during a storm. He knows that only a god can save him so he makes a deal with Nettuno (Neptune, god of the seas) that he will sacrifice the first living creature he comes across after he lands.

The first person Idomeneo sees is his own son Idamante. Idamante is a grown man in love with the beautiful Trojan prisoner Ilia. She is the daughter of Priam, the king of Troy. To make things more complicated, there is a Greek princess Electra who is also in love with Idamante and wants Ilia out of the way.

The King is very upset about having to sacrifice his son. He asks his counselor Arbace for advice, and they decide to have Idamante leave on a trip to escort Electra back home; that way he does not have to die per his father's deal with Nettuno. Idamante, unaware of his father's vow, gets on the boat with Electra but a terrible storm breaks and a sea monster appears — all caused by Nettuno, who is angry about the broken vow.

Idamante takes matters into his own hands and decides to fight the sea monster. While Idamante is off fighting the sea monster, Idomeneo confesses to his people that he struck a bargain with Nettuno that he cannot fulfill. Though Idamante defeats the monster, he nobly offers himself for sacrifice. But in that moment, Ilia offers herself for sacrifice in Idamante's place. Everyone, except Electra, is so moved by Idamante and Ilia's love they get a pardon from Nettuno. The god now agrees to bless their marriage if Idomeneo steps down as king in favor of Idamante and Ilia.

Electra falls into despair, but everyone else finds happiness.

IDOMENEO

ROMÉO ET JULIETTE
By Charles Gounod

b. June 17, 1818 in Paris, France
d. October 18, 1893 in Saint-Cloud (Paris), France
Premiered in 1867

Roméo et Juliette is based on William Shakespeare's tragedy, *Romeo and Juliet.* Juliette Capulet is a young girl in Verona, Italy during the thirteen hundreds. She is in love with Roméo Montague, a member of a rival family. Juliette has to meet Roméo in secret because her parents have already arranged a marriage for her to keep their family in power. Juliette's nurse acts as a go-between and helps them meet with a friar who believes in their love and marries them in secret. They hatch a plan to escape together but they cannot do it right away.

Unfortunately, Roméo and his Montague crowd, armed with knives, get into a street fight in downtown Verona. Tybalt kills Mercutio, a Montague, and then Roméo kills Tybalt, a Capulet. The Duke of Verona sends Roméo into exile. Before he leaves he sneaks over to Juliette's room to say goodbye.

Now it is time for Juliette to marry her designated husband Count Pâris. The problem is that the nurse and the friar know she is already married and they do not dare tell her parents. They convince Juliette to take a potion that will make her appear dead. The plan is that while she appears dead, Juliette will be carried down to the family tomb so that when she wakes up she can escape with Roméo.

Juliette drinks the potion as planned and everyone thinks she has died. Bad news travels fast and Roméo hears about her death. He does not know about the potion.

Roméo makes his way back to Verona to the Capulet tomb to say goodbye to Juliette before she is buried. He is so distraught at seeing her dead that he decides to drink poison so they can be united in death. Juliette starts to awaken just as Roméo starts to die. She takes his dagger and stabs herself and now they are together forever.

Aside: In the Middle Ages and the Renaissance, and sometimes even after, noble families would arrange marriages to make sure they stayed in power. The woes of arranged marriage are fodder for many operas, including others in this book like *Madama Butterfly* and *Lucia di Lammermoor*!

KÁT'A (KATYA) KABANOVÁ
by Leoš Janáčcek

b. July 3, 1854 in Hukvaldy, Czech Republic
d. August 10, 1928 in Ostrava, Czech Republic
Premiered in 1921

Kát'a Kabanová, sometimes spelled *Katya Kabanová*, is a dramatic opera from the Modern/Twentieth-Century era. Katya is a young Russian woman married to a man named Tichon. They live on a farm on the banks of the Volga River in the mid-eighteen hundreds. Kabanicha, Katya's mother-in-law, has it out for her. She constantly criticizes Katya, and Tichon for not being stricter with his young wife. They are caught in a loveless marriage.

Luckily Katya is very close to Kabanicha's foster daughter Varvara. She is Katya's only friend. Varvara notices Katya's misery, but also notices that Katya is a beautiful person. She encourages her to seek happiness. In fact, Varvara notices a young man named Boris smiling at Katya.

Apparently Kabanicha notices this too, and accuses Katya of all sorts of infamy while her son is away on business. Katya and Boris fall in love. When Tichon returns from his trip, he is furious because he cares for Katya, even if there is no passion in their marriage. The two lovers try to give each other up and Katya returns to Tichon.

There is a powerful summer storm. Katya can no longer take the misery that her mother-in-law and husband cause her. Knowing that she can never be with Boris, she throws herself in the Volga River.

Boris's uncle pulls Katya's lifeless body from the river. Tichon accuses his mother of having pushed Katya over the edge. Kabanicha thanks Dikoy for retrieving Katya's body.

Aside: In this opera, Kabanicha represents the old-time Russian matriarch who acts as an informal head of the family. Part of this opera's drama is the conflict between the old ways and the new ways that Varvara and Katya try to enact.[4]

KATYA KABANOVA

KATYA KABANOVA-JANACEK-The MATRIARCH pushes her daughter in law over the edge, into the VOLGA

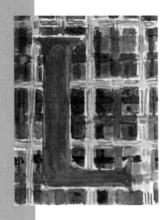

LUCIA DI LAMMERMOOR
By Gaetano Donizetti

b. November 29, 1797 in Bergamo, Italy
d. April 8, 1848 in Bergamo, Italy
Premiered in 1839

Lucia di Lammermoor is a tragic opera based on a story by Sir Walter Scott called *The Bride of Lammermoor* that takes place in Scotland. Because the composer was Italian everyone has Italian names and sings in Italian. Lucia is a young Scottish woman who is in love with Edgardo, her brother's sworn enemy. They must meet in secret out in the Lammermoor park.

One moonlit night Lucia and her companion Alisa are walking in the park when Edgardo comes to find her to say he has to go to France. They exchange rings as a sign of their love. In the meantime, Lucia's controlling brother Enrico has discovered his sister's secret liaison and tries to end it so he can marry her off to the nobleman Arturo. Not only is there a generations-old feud with Edgardo's family, marrying her to Arturo will advance his own aims. To convince Lucia the affair is over, he intercepts the letters from Edgardo and substitutes forged ones that make her think he no longer loves her.

This distressing news makes Lucia more willing to marry Arturo. Enrico preys on her vulnerable state by convincing her that marrying Arturo will be better for their family. Lucia tries to seek counsel from the family chaplain but he is on her brother's side and offers no solace.

Even though Lucia thinks Edgardo betrayed her, she still loves him. In fact, Arturo wonders why Lucia is so morose. Enrico blames her mood on mourning for their late mother. Lucia and Arturo sign the marriage contract in front of family and friends. As they celebrate, Edgardo returns and discovers Lucia exchanging wedding vows with Arturo. Enrico has betrayed them both.

Enrico challenges Edgardo to a duel at dawn in the churchyard where Edgardo's relatives are buried. The chaplain finds Lucia upstairs, covered with blood — she has killed her husband and gone insane. He comes downstairs to tell the guests the shocking news when Lucia appears in her bloody white nightgown and sings her famous mad scene. The emotional stress causes her to fall and die, and the disturbed guests leave. They meet Edgardo in the churchyard, and when he finds out she is dead, he stabs himself.

Aside: The famous mad scene is one of the most difficult pieces in opera to perform correctly. The performer must not only strike the right balance of sadness and insanity, but also sing in tune with a flute at the same time!

MEFISTOFELE
by Arrigo Boito

b. February 24, 1842 in Padua, Italy
d. June 10, 1918 in Milan, Italy
Premiered in 1868

Mefistofele is the devil incarnate. His partner in crime is an old German doctor named Faust, who is tired of his humdrum life. Mefistofele appears in the doctor's study and offers to serve him on Earth and fulfill his every desire in exchange for the doctor's soul when he dies.

Mefistofele turns Faust into a young man again, and Faust pursues the beautiful maiden Margherita. He convinces Margherita to give a sleeping potion to her mother so they can be together. Then Faust and Mefistofele leave for Brocken, a mountain in Germany, and meet dancing witches.

Margherita is sent to jail, accused of poisoning her mother with the sleeping potion, and of drowning her baby. Faust and Mefistofele appear in jail and Faust begs Mefistofele for help so he can save Margherita. Mefistofele opens the prison door, but Margherita sees the devil and refuses to go with her rescuers. She asks God for forgiveness and dies, her soul saved. The doctor and the demon escape.

Faust and Mefistofele continue on to other infamous places. They party with fallen and disgraced heroes. Faust meets Helen of Troy, over whom the Trojan War began, on a magical island and falls in love with her. Mefistofele arranges this so he can entrap Faust as a companion in his evil deeds. It would be hard for Faust to give up such a lifestyle of worldly temptations.

In the end, however, Faust comes to his senses. In the epilogue, Mefistofele visits the doctor, who is old again and dying. This time, Faust is able to resist the temptation and prays to heaven to die instead, which he does. In the end, even Faust wants the good forces to succeed over evil.

Aside: The kind of bargain that Mefistofele and Faust forge is known as a "Faustian bargain" or a "deal with the devil." The plot to this opera is based on a very famous fable, *Faust*, written by the German philosopher Johann Wolfgang von Goethe (**gu**-*tah*). There are several ballets and operas named for Faust that involve the bargain-with-the-devil theme. *Mefistofele* contains the same idea as *Faust* except it puts more of the spotlight on the devil.

Mefisto fele
Faust

Mefistofele - A. Boito - The Devil's take on
Goethe's FAUST - Margurite, Martin de Oi...

NORMA
by Vincenzo Bellini

b. November 3, 1801 in Catania, Italy
d. September 23, 1835 in Puteaux, France
Premiered in 1831

Norma is often considered the epitome of the **bel canto** tradition with its recognizable arias. This opera is set in Gaul (now France) during the Roman occupation around 50 BCE. At this time, the Druid people lived there. Norma is a Druid high priestess and daughter of Oroveso, the head priest.

Norma has a secret relationship with Pollione (**poh**-*lee-oh-neh*), the Roman proconsul. Although having a relationship with a Roman person is a crime punishable to burn at the stake, Norma and the proconsul have two children together. Lately the relationship has been rocky because Pollione is now in love with Adalgisa, a Druid priestess. Norma senses this.

One night Norma is at her house feeling sorry for herself and her two children. She knows it is over with Pollione but does not know his new love interest's identity. Adalgisa, who admires and loves the older high priestess, comes to ask Norma's advice. Should she escape with the Roman who loves her, confess her love for him and leave behind her faith and people? For a moment Norma thinks of her own plight. All of a sudden, Pollione appears and Norma realizes that he is the Roman that Adalgisa was talking about.

Norma is so distraught that she considers killing her children, but then changes her mind and decides she will give up Pollione if Adalgisa agrees to become a mother to her children. Adalgisa refuses and insists that Pollione do his duty as a father and stay with Norma and the children. Adalgisa renounces Pollione and returns to her life as a priestess in the temple.

Norma tries to rally the Druids to war against the Romans, but there is a huge ruckus coming from the temple that distracts them. It turns out that Pollione has broken into the sacred Druid temple attempting to kidnap Adalgisa and take her to Rome. It is punishable by death for a nonbeliever to enter the temple.

Norma tries to save Pollione and in doing so, reveals her lasting, clandestine love. The Druids apprehend him and bring him before the priest for trespassing. She marches up the funeral pyre to die with him. He realizes he loves Norma after all and follows her into the flames.

Aside: The Druids occupied parts of Europe before Judaism, Christianity and Islam were introduced. They worshipped elements of nature.

NORMA BELLIONI Addgis

ORFEO ED EURIDICE
by Christoph Willibald Gluck

b. July 2, 1714 in Berching, Germany
d. November 15, 1787 in Vienna, Austria
Premiered in 1762

Orfeo ed Euridice is an opera based on the Greek myth of Orpheus and Eurydice, the great musician and his lost love. Orfeo could charm all living creatures with his music. When his beloved wife Euridice (*e-yu-reh-**dee**-che*) dies from a poisonous snakebite, it sends him into deep despair.

He begs Zeus, the ruler of the gods, to bring Euridice back to life. Zeus hears his pleas. Amore, the god of love, comes to lead Orfeo to Hades, the god of the underworld to whom all souls go after death. Amore tells Orfeo that he may retrieve his wife and lead her back across the river Styx to the world of the living. There is one condition: Orfeo must not look at Euridice until their journey is completed or she will die immediately.

Orfeo uses his musical powers to lead himself safely through the underworld. He meets many dangerous creatures like Cerberus the three-headed watchdog, and the Erinyes, goddesses who punished criminals. He charms them all with song and so they let him pass.

Finally, Orfeo arrives at the Elysian Fields where the good spirits spend eternity. There, he finds Euridice. As he leads her out of Hades, she wonders why he will not look at her. She worries that he no longer loves her. Euridice does not know about the deal Orfeo made with Amore. She cries and begs him to look at her. Orfeo struggles to resist her but he cannot. He looks at her to explain, and she dies a second time.

In response, Orfeo sings his most beautiful songs, "Cosa faro' senza Euridice" ("What Will I Do Without Euridice?"). This proves his love and grief for Euridice. The gods are so touched that Amore appears and restores her to life.

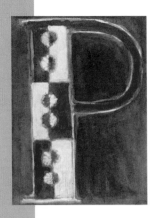

PAGLIACCI
by Ruggiero Leoncavallo

b. April 23, 1857 in Naples, Italy
d. August 9, 1919 in Montecatini Terme, Italy
Premiered in 1892

Pagliacci (**pah**-*lyat-chee*), or "clowns" in Italian, falls into the *verismo* genre. In this case, the realistic setting is a tumultuous backdrop of circus wagons and tents. This opera is about a troupe of minstrels performing a play in the small southern Italian town of Montalto, Calabria, during the mid-eighteen hundreds. The cast is small and the story takes place in a very short time frame.

Canio is the head clown. Nedda, his wife, is also a clown but she wants out of the troupe – she plans to run off with Silvio, a local villager. Tonio and Beppe round out the troupe. Tonio is attracted to Nedda, but she spurns him. Tonio and Canio team up to expose Nedda's secret lover and thwart her escape.

That night, the tension escalates as Canio, dressed as the character Pagliaccio, tricks Nedda, dressed as Columbine, into saying her lover's name. Nedda cries out his name as she tries to flee from Canio. The audience within the story is watching all of this and thinking it is part of the performance.

On stage, Canio takes a knife and stabs Nedda. Silvio jumps on the stage to save her and gets killed, too. As a dazed Canio drops the knife, he speaks the last line: "La commedia e finita," or "The comedy is over."

Aside: At first, Leoncavallo was accused of plagiarism by one of his contemporaries who had based a play on a similar story. Leoncavallo was able to fight the charges by proving that, when he was a boy, his father was the judge who presided over the murder trial of a jealous actor who killed his wife and her lover.[5]

DON QUICHOTTE
by Jules Massenet

b. May 12, 1842 in Montaud, France
d. August 13, 1912 in Paris, France
Premiered in 1910

Don Quichotte is an opera based on Miguel de Cervantes' classic *Don Quixote*, written in 1605 in Spain. To understand the opera one has to know who Don Quichotte is.

Don Quichotte is an ageing, impoverished nobleman who spends his days reading books about knights saving ladies and performing other heroic acts. One day he believes he is one of these noble knights when in reality he is a tired man living in a dream world. He buys an old nag of a horse and sets off across the countryside to protect the poor, widows and orphans. He finds himself a bumbling sidekick, Sancho Panza, who helps him on his missions — tasks that become fools' errands, like fighting windmills that he thinks are giants. People mock him everywhere he goes, but he is oblivious.

In the opera, he is in love with Dulcinée, a woman with many suitors. When Don Quichotte and Sancho are below her balcony he throws kisses to her while everyone around him makes fun of his appearance. He is a wizened old man on a nag with a bowl on his head for a helmet who thinks he is a dashing young knight. Dulcinée does come to her balcony to acknowledge him, at least. He is a local legend of sorts. Don Quichotte has heard that someone stole her favorite pearl necklace. He vows to get it back for her.

Don Quichotte sends Sancho ahead to scout out the bandits. Sancho thinks this is just another harebrained idea. In the meantime, Don Quichotte goes off to fight some windmills that he thinks are giants.

The bandits end up finding them and when they do, Don Quichotte gives them a speech that takes them aback. He describes his missions as the errant knight, only out to help the poor and right wrongs. The bandits give back the jewelry, mystically overcome by his sincerity.

Don Quichotte proudly returns with Dulcinée's necklace. She is thrilled and to show how happy she is, she gives him a kiss. Don Quichotte is ecstatic and proposes marriage. Everyone who witnesses this ridicules him, though Dulcinée lets him down gently.

Don Quichotte goes on his way, exhausted but pleased with his good deed. He and Sancho stop to rest against a tree. Don Quichotte sits down, looks up at the starry sky and dies a happy man.

DON QUIXOTE

Don Quixote - Jules Massenet - Dulcinea 1†† requests her long Lost necklace from the DON

RIGOLETTO
by Giuseppe Verdi

b. October 10, 1813 in Le Roncole, Italy
d. January 27, 1901 in Milan, Italy
Premiered in 1851

Rigoletto is one of the major defining works of the grand opera tradition. Rigoletto is the name of the hunchback jester in the court of the Duke of Mantua, Italy. The opera takes place during the Renaissance when Italy was broken down into many dukedoms. The Duke's court is full of noblemen, and he flirts with their wives while Rigoletto makes fun of the jealous husbands. This does not win Rigoletto many fans.

Among the Duke's enemies is the old Count of Monterone, who publicly accuses the Duke of dishonoring his daughter. The Count curses the Duke, as well as Rigoletto for mocking him. *La maledizione*, or the curse, terrifies Rigoletto.

Rigoletto has a daughter Gilda whom nobody in the court knows about. One day the Duke, dressed in plain clothes, spots Gilda at church and follows her home. He tells Gilda he is a poor student and that he loves her, and Gilda falls in love with him.

Meanwhile, several nobles follow Rigoletto home and think Gilda is his secret lover. To get revenge for all his taunting, they decide to abduct her and take her to the Duke's palace. The nobles blindfold Rigoletto and trick him into thinking he is helping abduct a different woman for the Duke, when it is in fact his own daughter! Once Rigoletto realizes this, he is determined to seek vengeance.

Rigoletto hires a local thug called Sparafucile (**Spah**-*rah-foo-chee-leh*) to kill the Duke. They hatch a plan to use Sparafucile's sister, the pretty Maddalena, to lure the Duke to a secluded spot so Sparafucile can kill him. However, Maddalena is taken by the Duke's good looks and gets her brother to spare him. Since he is a contract killer, Sparafucile agrees to kill the next person to knock on the door, and give the body in a sack to Rigoletto when he returns with the rest of his payment.

Gilda overhears these plans. Because she loves the Duke, she decides to sacrifice herself for him. She knocks on the door and gets stabbed and wrapped in a sack for Rigoletto. Rigoletto tears open the sack and realizes the curse has been actualized: the Duke is still alive and Gilda is dying. As she says goodbye to her beloved father, Rigoletto's final words of the opera are "La maledizione!"

RIGOLETTO

Rigoletto, jester, single Dad of Gilda. Gilda, tricked by Duke of Mantova & then, kidnapped 4 the Duke by Dinald & his enemies. Sparafucile offers R his services. MALEDIZIONE

SALOME
by Richard Strauss

b. June 11, 1864 in Munich, Germany
d. September 8, 1949 in Garmisch-Partenkirchen, Germany
Premiered in 1905

Salome (sa-low-may) is a bible story turned into an opera. The main characters are Salome and Jokanaan (John the Baptist). The opera takes place around the year 30 in Galilee, Judea (now Israel), at King Herodes' palace.

Salome is Herodes' stepdaughter. Herodias, her mother, is a cold, calculating woman who killed her husband to become Herodes' queen. The depraved palace life has rubbed off on the young Salome.

When Salome sees the imprisoned Jokanaan, she starts flirting with him. He is in jail for trying to convert the people of Galilee to Christianity. Salome ramps up her solicitations: she tells Jokanaan she wants to touch his skin and hair, and kiss his lips. Narraboth, a young palace guard in love with Salome witnesses this and cannot bear it. He kills himself in despair. Salome is oblivious and Jokanaan disapproves of her terrible behavior.

Herodes is obsessed with Salome, and she knows it. As the evening wears on, he wants to see Salome do a dance with her veils. Salome does not feel like it. Herodes keeps pleading and she finally agrees to dance if he will grant her a wish that she will reveal after her dance. He agrees to her demands.

Salome starts her famous dance of the seven veils. When she is done, she demands Jokanaan's head. His rejection offends her, to say the least. The last thing Herodes wants to do is have Jokanaan beheaded — it would cause a revolution in his kingdom — but Salome drives a hard bargain. Because he is a weak and depraved man, he gives in to Salome.

Jokanaan is beheaded in his dungeon. His head is presented to Salome on a silver platter. When she sees it, she dances frantically, talking to the head as if were alive and kissing its lips. Herodes, shocked and disgusted, has Salome executed on the spot.

Aside: The phrase "the dance of the seven veils" is now a metaphor for holding out and acting disinterested as a way to achieve one's goal.

SALOME - R. Strauss - not the
average Bible story -

TURANDOT
by Giacomo Puccini

b. December 22, 1858 in Lucca, Italy
d, November 29, 1924 in Brussels, Belgium
Premiered in 1926

Turandot was unfinished at the time of Puccini's death but became a part of the twentieth-century operatic tradition nonetheless. Turandot is a cruel Chinese princess who lives in ancient China. Though she is cold, she has many suitors. In order to marry her, suitors must solve three riddles that she creates. Those who fail are put to death, yet would-be suitors come from around the world to try. Calaf is one of them. Calaf's father is Timur, the banished king of Tartary, a large region of Asia. Timur is blind and traveling with his loyal servant girl Liù. Calaf is surprised to run into them in the crowd gathered before Turandot's palace. Everyone is waiting to hear the verdict on the latest suitor.

Calaf decides that he is going to try to solve Turandot's riddle because he is in love with her. Liù and his father beg him not to try for fear he will be executed like all the contestants before him. As he makes his way to the palace, a trio of ministers named Ping, Pang and Pong try to warn him. Calaf is relentless and presents himself to the icy princess. Even she warns him before starting but he insists he is ready to live or die for her. To everyone's amazement, Calaf answers all three riddles. Turandot is shocked that she has to keep up her part of the bargain and marry Calaf. Her father the Emperor says she must keep her promise.

Calaf cuts her a break and says that if Turandot can guess his name by the following dawn he will offer himself for execution. She sends out her troops to discover his identity when Timur and Liù are spotted talking to him. Turandot threatens torture but they stay mum. Liù kills herself to avoid telling Calaf's name because she loves him too and wants him to live. Turandot's cruelty shocks Calaf but still he takes her in his arms and tries to kiss her. At first she resists, but then she realizes she loves him. Calaf finally reveals his true identity as the prince of Tartary and offers his life, so it is up to Turandot to decide if he lives or dies. Turandot announces to the awaiting crowd that she has guessed the stranger's name, and it is… Love! The crowd cheers for the lovers.

Aside: The aria "Nessun dorma" ("No One Sleeps") from this opera was used as the theme song for the 1990 World Cup and during the opening ceremony of the 2006 Winter Olympics. The famous tenor Luciano Pavarotti (1935-2007) sang this song at both sporting events.

Turindot-Puccini- Calaf, son of exiled king of Tartary is ready to die for the ♡ of Princess Turindot

IL RITORNO D'ULISSE IN PATRIA
by Claudio Monteverdi

b. May 15, 1567 in Cremona, Italy
d. November 29, 1643 in Venice, Italy
Premiered in 1641

Il Ritorno d'Ulisse in Patria (Ulysses' Return Home) is one of the famous operas of the Baroque era. It is based on the hero Ulisse's return home after ten years fighting the Trojan War and another ten traveling back to his native Ithaca, a Greek island. When he returns, nobody recognizes him until Minerva, the goddess of wisdom, appears just in time to help him reclaim his wife Penelope and his palace.

Penelope has been waiting all these years for Ulisse to return. Presumed a widow, Penelope keeps at bay numerous suitors by promising to choose a new husband when she finishes her weaving. Penelope secretly unravels her day's work of weaving every night when she is alone.

News reaches the palace that Ulisse is coming and may even be among them now. Who knows what he looks like after so many years away? Ulisse's servant is the only one who recognizes him as an old man in disguise.

The last four suitors hear this and start pressuring Penelope to pick one of them. Telemaco arrives with the disguised Ulisse just in time. The suitors make fun of this seemingly elderly man. Ulisse beats one of them up in a wrestling match and impresses Penelope with his strength.

Penelope produces Ulisse's bow and says she will marry the man who can shoot an arrow with it. Everyone fails but Ulisse succeeds, and then he turns and shoots arrows at the suitors.

Everyone in the family except for Penelope recognizes the old man as Ulisse. Luckily Ericlea, Penelope's long time attendant, recognizes the scar on Ulisse's back and points it out. Penelope is hard to convince but in the end she realizes that this old man really is Ulisse, and they are joyfully reunited.

Il Ritorno di Ulisse - very early opera by Montiverdi.
Penelope is @ loom, nurse Ericlea fend off Penelope's suitors, when

VANESSA
by Samuel Barber

b. March 9, 1910 in Chester, PA
d. January 23, 1981 in New York City, New York
Premiered in 1958

Vanessa is a dramatic opera set in early nineteen hundreds. Vanessa lives in her ancestral home with her mother, a baroness, and Erika, her niece. They have just received word that Anatol, the only man has Vanessa ever loved, is coming to visit. Vanessa was so devastated when they split up that she covered all the mirrors in the house so she would not see herself age.

The visitor who arrives is not Vanessa's former lover, but his son, also named Anatol. Vanessa is disappointed and leaves young Anatol and Erika to have dinner together.

A month goes by and Anatol has fallen in love with Erika. He proposes marriage, but Erika is unsure. Vanessa, delusional, has fallen for Anatol, too. She is determined to have him for herself. Vanessa will only uncover the mirrors if he will love her. Erika tries to explain to Vanessa that she has mistaken his identity and that young Anatol really loves her, not Vanessa.

Erika gets her grandmother the Baroness on her side, but Vanessa has managed to win over her beloved Anatol. At the New Year's Eve ball, Vanessa and Anatol's engagement is announced. Upon hearing this, Erika has a huge meltdown and faints. When she wakes up, she runs outside and vanishes.

Vanessa worries about her niece and is relieved when Anatol finds her alive. Vanessa and Anatol marry and Erika stays in the big old house with the Baroness, bitter and abandoned. Like Vanessa did years ago when Anatol jilted her, Erika covers up all the mirrors so she will not see herself age. It is now Erika's turn to wait.

Vanessa – by S. Barber   a story of unrequited love & mistaken I.D.

DIE WALKÜRE
by Richard Wagner

b. May 22, 1813 in Leipzig, Germany
d. February 13, 1883 in Venice, Italy
Premiered in 1862

Die Walküre (The Valkyrie) is the second opera in Richard Wagner's epic *Der Ring des Nibelungen* (Ring Cycle). This cycle contains four operas that are based on ancient German mythology. The gods in this mythology live in Valhalla, which is like Mount Olympus in Greek mythology.

In the first opera, many Germanic tribes are fighting. The head god Wotan controls one of these tribes. The Valkyries are Wotan's eight daughters: goddesses with superior powers. Wotan also has mortal children, including the twins Siegmund and Sieglinde. One of the warring factions, led by Hunding, captures Sieglinde and forces her to marry him.

Years later, Siegmund shows up at Sieglinde's hut in the woods. Sieglinde invites the stranger inside. They do not recognize each other as brother and sister. When Hunding comes home, he discovers the stranger is from the Walses, the enemy tribe. He tells Siegmund he is allowed to spend the night, but that they must battle each other the next day. Siegmund recalls a promise his father Wotan once made: that he would give him a sword in his greatest moment of need.

Sieglinde gives Hunding a sleeping potion and tells Siegmund the story of her wedding, when a stranger buried a sword deep into the trunk of an ash tree, and nobody has been able to get it out since. Because Sigmund is Wotan's son, he is able to pull it out! Siegmund and Sieglinde escape, hoping to stay together.

Unfortunately, this plan angers the goddess Fricka, who is guardian of the marriage vow. Wotan wants to send Brünnhilde, his favorite daughter, to save Siegmund and Sieglinde but Fricka insists the marriage between Hunding and Sieglinde must be respected. Frustrated, Wotan orders Brünnhilde to do as Fricka wishes and make sure Siegmund dies.

Brünnhilde tries to warn Siegmund and offers to save him, but he refuses to leave Sieglinde. Moved by his courage, Brünnhilde decides to defy her father's orders: she will now help Siegmund win. Hunding arrives to fight Siegmund and at first it seems Siegmund will win, but Wotan steps in and destroys Siegmund's sword. Defenseless, Hunding kills him. Brünnhilde escapes with Sieglinde and goes to hide with her sisters, the Valkyries. Wotan must now punish Brünnhilde. She lies down on a sacred rock where a ring of magic fire surrounds her. She is to lie inside the ring, asleep and powerless, until a hero can rescue her.

Die Walküre — Wagner's Ring Cycle — 4 operas
many plots — Brünhild & Fricka comes down Wotan
Brünhilde goes out in a ring of fire

XERSE
by Francesco Cavalli

b. February 14, 1602 in Crema, Italy
January 14, 1676 in Venice, Italy
Premiered in 1654

Xerse (Xerxes) is an opera based on the real tyrannical King Xerxes of Persia, well known for his epic battles with Greece. In the opera, Xerse is portrayed not as the famous military figure who invaded Greece, but as a fictionalized player in an entangled love debacle.

One day Xerse is out in his garden, singing to his favorite tree—an unexpected pastime for a tyrant king. He does not notice that the young Romilda has caught him singing. She finds it amusing that even he is a victim of love. Xerse falls in love with Romilda, even though he is already engaged to the foreign princess Amastre. Romilda, however, loves Arsamene, Xerse's brother. Romilda's sister Adelanta also loves Arsamene.

Xerse banishes Arsamene from his kingdom because they are both in love with Romilda. Romilda spurns Xerse's love overtures. Then Princess Amastre, who is supposed to marry Xerse, arrives disguised as a military general with a big beard. She does this so she can be close to palace intrigue.

Arsamene sends a love letter to Romilda with his servant Elviro, but Princess Amastre convinces him to give the letter to Adelanta instead. Adelanta shows the letter to Xerse, making him think Arsamene loves her, and not Romilda. Adelanta also tells Arsamene's servant Elviro that Romilda has chosen Xerse, even though this is not true. Arsamene is shocked. All characters delve into the jealous confusion that Adelanta's scheme creates. Eventually, Romilda and Arsamene catch Adelanta and make her confess her plot. When Xerse threatens to kill Arsamene, Romilda agrees to marry Xerse to save the man she loves.

Luckily, another misunderstanding works in the lovers' favor. Xerse tells Romilda's father that she must marry a man from his family. The father consents and begins planning a wedding. Xerse goes to get ready, while the father prepares for what he thinks is a wedding for Romilda and Arsamene. While Xerse is off primping, Romilda and Arsamene get married and Xerse shows up to find that they have wed. He is enraged. Suddenly Amastre, who has been in disguise, reveals herself and her lasting love for Xerse. Touched by her faithfulness, Xerse becomes ashamed of his infidelity and pledges himself to her. Only the devious Adelanta is left alone.

Aside: In Persepolis, Iran, there are actual bas reliefs, or sculptures carved into flat surfaces that do not stand on their own, that depict Xerxes in his historical military endeavors.

XORXES

XERXES - Handel's opera set in ancient
Persia - Xerxes is in ♥ us w/ Romilda who sees Xerxes

YEVGENY ONEGIN
by Pyotr Ilyich Tchaikovsky

b. May 7, 1840 in Votkinsk, Russia
d. November 6, 1893 in Saint Petersburg, Russia
Premiered in 1879

*Yevgeny Onegin (yev-**geh**-nee oh-**niyay**-gin)* is based on Alexander Pushkin's famous Russian poem of the same name. Yevgeny is Russian for "Eugene." This lyric drama is often billed as *Eugene Onegin*. It takes place in Saint Petersburg, Russia in the late seventeen hundreds.

The opera opens with Tatiana and her older sister Olga out in the garden when Lenski, Olga's fiancée, arrives with his dashing young friend, Yevgeny. Tatiana is instantly smitten with him. She is so infatuated that she stays up all night and composes a love letter describing her feelings. Tatiana gets her governess to deliver the letter.

The next day they are out in the garden again. Tatiana sees Yevgeny and realizes that sending him the letter was not a good idea. He rejects her and tells her he only has brotherly feelings for her. She is humiliated.

Soon, there is a big party for Tatiana's birthday. Things are a little tense between Lenski and Yevgeny so Yevgeny starts causing trouble between the fiancés. He cuts in during dances, flirts and goes out of his way to make things uncomfortable. As was the custom for the eighteenth-century Russian elite, Lenski challenges Yevgeny to a duel. That puts a damper on the party.

The next day at dawn the two former friends meet for the duel. Yevgeny kills Lenski, who dies declaring his love for Olga.

Years later, there is a ball in a beautiful house in Saint Petersburg. The house belongs to Prince Gremin and Tatiana, his lovely wife. It is the same Tatiana, now a grown woman. Yevgeny is among the ball guests. When he realizes his stunning hostess is none other than Tatiana, the tables turn and now he is the one in love.

Tatiana recognizes him and grants Yevgeny an audience alone. He pleads his love for her. This time it is she who rejects him. She goes back to join her beloved husband and leaves Yevgeny alone.

58

EVGENY ONEGIN

Yevgeny Onegin - Tchaikovsky's opera based on Pushkin's poem. Tchaikovsky started with Tatyana's letter aria. The rest is from the heart.

DIE ZAUBERFLÖTE
by Wolfgang Amadeus Mozart

b. January 27, 1756 in Salzburg, Austria
d. September 5, 1791 in Vienna, Austria
Premiered in 1791

Die Zauberflöte (The Magic Flute) is an important opera in many ways. This is the first opera that was written for people of all social classes. Because it clearly supported the right of individuals to pursue their own happiness, it raised eyebrows when it debuted. The main characters are Papageno and Papagena (both bird-catchers), Tamino, Pamina, Königin der Nacht (Queen of the Night), Sarastro the high priest, and Monostatos the villain.

Die Zauberflöte is based on an ancient fairy tale that takes place in Egypt. Pamina, Königin der Nacht's daughter, is gone! Sarastro, the high priest of the gods Osiris and Isis, has kidnapped her. Königin der Nacht enlists Papageno, her bird-catcher, and Tamino the prince to find her. Königin der Nacht's three handmaidens show Tamino a picture of Pamina. He is smitten and ready to go with Papageno on this quest to rescue Pamina. The handmaidens give Tamino a magic flute, and Papageno magic chimes that will protect them against evil powers.

They get to Pamina just in time! When they find her, the evil Monostatos is harassing her. At Sarastro's temple a high priest tells Tamino that Sarastro is not evil, and that he is a wise and noble man. It is the Königin der Nacht who is evil! Sarastro helps Tamino and Papageno free Pamina from Monostatos. Tamino and Pamina find each other and fall in love.

Papageno feels left out and wishes he could find a mate like Tamino does. An elderly woman appears asking for help. When Papageno helps her, she turns into a beautiful young woman Papagena, who is also a bird-catcher. There are more obstacles that Tamino and Pamina have to overcome in order to find their destined happiness.

Königin der Nacht has teamed up with the wicked Monostatos to get revenge on Sarastro. They have come to destroy Sarastro's temple but they fail. Night is turned into day, Königin der Nacht and Monostatos are vanquished, and everyone lives happily ever after.

Aside: *Die Zauberflöte* was Mozart's last opera. It was first performed two months before he died on September 30, 1791. Mozart was very involved with Freemasonry, an organization with rites going back to ancient Egypt. Freemasonry was a hot topic in Mozart's time.[6]

Die Zauber Flöte   Muzart's last opera
                                    The Magic Flute
Papageno Tamina Queen of the Night. Zorastro - Free Masons

RESOURCES

If you are interested in any of these stories, there are many opportunities to see the operas in this book and more.

Most major cities and even some smaller ones have opera houses, or feature opera performances in other venues like concert halls. You can check your local opera house or concert hall for performances in your area. Many of these venues, such as the Metropolitan Opera House in New York City, New York, also have informative websites that you can visit to find video clips and audio samples.

Live performances that have been filmed are available online through other websites. If you enter the name of an opera into a search engine, in its original language or in translation, you will find links to video clips of various scenes from the opera and, sometimes, the entire opera.

You can rent or buy film versions of operas on video as well. *Carmen, Die Zauberflöte, Don Giovanni, Yevgeny Onegin* and *Madama Butterfly* have all been made into feature films.

If you get a chance to see an opera, live or filmed, here are some terms that you read about in this book or might come across that will help you as you continue to explore opera.

Key Terms

opera- a work of art that combines words and music, along with other dramatic elements like costumes and sets, that began effectively in the sixteen hundreds

libretto- the words to the opera

score- the music to the opera

overture- a song that the orchestra plays at the beginning of an opera that usually contains parts of all of the songs featured

aria- an operatic melody for one person

duet- an operatic melody for two people

harpsichord- an instrument with strings inside that the player plucks by pressing a keyboard like a piano, but with a different sound; developed before the piano

chorus- a group of singers that was featured in later operas

buffoon- a character like a clown or jester, meant to amuse; often the brunt of the comedy in *opera buffa*

habanera- a style of Cuban dance music with a characteristic rhythm that developed in the early eighteen hundreds; a piece of music written in this style

aside- when one character in the opera speaks directly to the audience to tell them something the rest of the characters cannot hear

recitative- an instance of speaking in opera, ranging from rhythmically spoken words to words spoken melodically to music, that was common during the early years of opera especially during the Baroque period

bel canto, "beautiful singing"- a term that became associated with opera during the Classical era; can refer to an elaborate style of singing, or complicated melodies that singers could embellish with their own flourishes, combined with musical numbers to create scenes

Major Eras

These four eras or periods are widely recognized as classifications in Classical music history. The dates are not exact, and certainly some scholars would place the beginning or end of an era differently. The dates listed below are commonly accepted and should function as useful guidelines for contextualizing the development of opera.

Baroque era- (1600-1750); Baroque operas featured arias and small orchestras that usually had a harpsichord

Classical era- (1750-1830); Classical operas featured larger orchestras, increasingly elaborate compositions and lavish stage spectacle

Romantic era- (1830-1900); Romantic operas evolved to be simpler than most Classical operas with more focus on singing and realistic stories

Modern/Twentieth-Century- (1900-present); early Modern opera integrated characteristics of previous eras but developed to contain more contemporary or innovative themes and styles

Genre

There are many different genres, or types of operas. Within the genres, there are more specific subgenres. Many operas have elements of more than one genre, so classifications are not always absolute. Something can be a grand opera and also an *opera seria* or a lyric drama that is also a fairy tale opera. For example, *Don Giovanni* has elements of *opera seria* and *opera buffa*. Some of the common genres and distinctions are listed below.

grand opera- a type of opera, tragic or comic, that usually features a large orchestra, lavish music and elaborate sets such as *Rigoletto*; sometimes features recitative in a form that is closer to singing than talking; can include ballet; does not contain spoken dialogue; developed during the Classical era

drame lyrique, or lyric drama- a simplified version of grand opera that could be tragic, dramatic or comic such as *Yevgeny Onegin*; developed during the Romantic era

opéra comique, or comic opera- an opera that is tragic or comedic but with some spoken dialogue and arias (not to be confused with *opera buffa*), such as *Carmen*; developed during the Classical era

opera seria- a serious opera usually based on mythology, religion or other related topics such as *Idomeneo*; developed during the Baroque era

opera buffa- an opera with more lighthearted or comic themes that often featured buffoons as the brunt of the comedy such as *Le Nozze di Figaro* or *Il barbiere di Siviglia*; developed during the Baroque era

verismo opera- an opera based on real-life characters or situations such *Pagliacci*; developed during the late Romantic and early Modern/Twentieth-Century eras

fairy tale opera- an opera based on a fairy tale such as *Hänsel und Gretel*

Voice

What defines a vocal type is much more complicated than whether a voice sounds high or low. However, when you are listening to opera or reading a program that lists characters by their voices, it will be helpful to have a very basic understanding of some of the major vocal types.

countertenor- a male voice that can be a tenor or a baritone with a wider range

tenor- the highest male voice

baritone- the middle range male voice

bass-baritone- the lower-middle range male voice

bass- the lowest male voice

soprano- the highest female voice

mezzo-soprano- the middle range female voice and the most common

contralto- the lowest female voice

NOTES

1. John Rosselli, *The Life of Verdi* (Cambridge, UK: Cambridge University Press, 2000), 158-159.
2. Joyce Bourne, *Opera: The Great Composers and Their Masterworks* (London, UK: Mitchell Beazley, 2008), 539.
3. Daniel Goldmark, "*What's Opera, Doc?* and Cartoon Opera," in *Tunes for 'Toons: Music and the Hollywood Cartoon* (Berkeley, CA: University of California Press, 2005).
4. George Harewood and Antony Peattie. *The New Kobbé's Complete Opera Book*, 11th ed. (New York, NY: G.P. Putnam's Sons, 1997), 382.
5. Harewood and Peattie, *Kobbé's*, 413.
6. Harewood and Peattie, *Kobbé's*, 524. Jeremy Siepmann, *Mozart: His Life & Music* (Naperville, IL: Sourcebooks, 2006), 118.

BIBLIOGRAPHY

Bourne, Joyce. *Opera: The Great Composers and Their Masterworks*. London, UK: Mitchell Beazley, 2008.

Charlton, David, ed. *The Cambridge Companion to Grand Opera*. Cambridge, UK: Cambridge University Press, 2003.

Harewood, George and Peattie, Antony. *The New Kobbé's Complete Opera Book*, 11th ed. New York: G.P. Putnam's Sons, 1997. First published in 1922.

Glasser, Alfred, ed. *The Lyric Opera Companion: The History, Lore, and Stories of the World's Greatest Operas.* Kansas City: Andrews and McMeel, 1991.

Goldmark, Daniel. "*What's Opera, Doc?* and Cartoon Opera," in *Tunes for 'Toons: Music and the Hollywood Cartoon*, University of California Press, 2005.

Holoman, D. Kern. *Evening With the Orchestra*. New York, NY: W.W. Norton, 1992.

Isacoff, Stuart. *A Natural History of the Piano: The Instrument, the Music, the Musicians from Mozart to Modern Jazz and Everything in Between*. New York, NY: Random House, 2011.

Jellinek, George. *History Through the Opera Glass: from the Rise of Caesar to the Fall of Napoleon*. New York, NY: Limelight, 2000. First published in 1994 by Kahn & Averill.

Landon, H.C. Robbins. "Mozart and His Audiences." Liner notes to Die Zauberflöte. Wolfgang Amadeus Mozart. CD. Decca, 1971.

Osborne, Charles. *The Opera Lover's Companion*. New Haven, CT: Yale University Press, 2004.

Rosselli, John. *The Life of Verdi*. Cambridge, UK: Cambridge University Press, 2000.

Sadie, Stanley. *Wagner and His Operas.* New York, NY: St. Martin's Press, 2000.

Steen, Michael. *The Lives & Times of the Great Composers.* New York, NY: Oxford University Press, 2004. First published in 2003 by Icon Books, Ltd.

Siepmann, Jeremy. *Mozart: His Life & Music.* Naperville, IL: Sourcebooks, 2006.

Young, John Bell. *Puccini: A Listener's Guide*. New York, NY: Amadeus Press, 2008.

INDEX

ABOUT THE ARTWORK

The original copyrighted artwork by Liddy Lindsay is watercolor on paper, 25".x 40". It is available as a Giclée print, a digital capture that is printed on German etching paper with archival ink. Each of the 26 letters of the English alphabet corresponds to the letter that starts the name of sequential operas or characters of operas, in original language, depicted in a 4".x7" format of a narrative scene incorporating the letter. In the four corner frames are portraits of Mozart, Verdi, Wagner and Puccini. "Opera A-Z" is both a visual learning tool and a work of art. It is an entrée into the magic of opera, a way for opera enthusiasts to share their love of the art form with the uninitiated, young and old alike.

CPSIA information can be obtained
at www.ICGtesting.com
Printed in the USA
BVXC01n1749020914
364756BV00002B/2